BRILLIANT
ON THE BASICS

A Playbook for Business Leaders

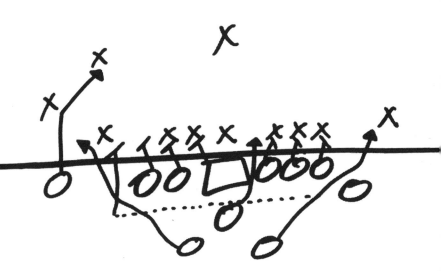

BARRY GOTTLIEB

ISBN: 1477690344
ISBN 13: 9781477690345

TABLE OF CONTENTS

INTRODUCTION

I began my career as an educator. First as an elementary school teacher, then as a principal, and then as an instructor at both Santa Fe Community College and the University of Florida.

Shortly after receiving my tenure, I left Gainesville and moved back to Miami to begin a whole new career in business.

Even though one of my partners was a tax attorney and the other partner had graduated from Georgia Tech, the three of us didn't really know very much about building a successful business.

This is when my "real education" began.

I made it my mission to study the best practices and principles of the top companies in the world. I read books, listened to tapes and CD's, attended seminars from some of the best business minds of the century, and found mentors that helped me to grow. I then applied what I had learned in our new business.

Over the next 22 years, my partners and I built a very successful $75M company that employed over 350 people. In 1998 we sold our company for $55M.

Since then, I have bought and sold interests in several companies. I continue to study the best practices and principles of the best companies in the world, and I use that knowledge to counsel and coach both private individuals and corporations.

This book is the compilation not only of the best practices and best principles that I learned from my mentors: Zig Ziglar – Wayne Dyer – Stephen Covey – Ed Foreman – Brian Tracy – Jack Welch – Denis Waitley – Buck Rogers – Chet Holmes – Harvey Mackay – Ken Blanchard – Earl Nightingale – Jack Canfield, but many, many more.

My sincere gratitude to them, and to all of my teachers, for the lessons they have shared.

My mission: To inspire and empower others to reach their full potential.

KNOWLEDGE IS POWER

"Knowing is not enough;
we must apply.
Willing is not enough;
we must do."

Johann Wolfgang Von Goethe

PREFACE

Knowledge is Power

In today's world, we have access to almost unlimited amounts of information with the touch of a keypad. You can find out about almost anything or anybody in just a few brief moments. The internet has made all of this possible, and with companies like Google, Bing, Facebook, Twitter and many others, we have access to an abundance of real time information.

Does all this knowledge give us power? I believe that most people would agree that it does. In my opinion, they are only partially correct. I believe that knowledge, in and of itself, has very little value. In order for knowledge to give us power, we must "apply" it.

Let me give you a glaring example of what I mean. We all know that cigarette smoking can and probably will kill us. Even with this knowledge, some people will continue to smoke. You are probably thinking that that it is a very hard habit to break and that is why most people don't quit. But what about all the people who have never smoked, and decide to start?

Here are other examples. People spend billions of dollars every year on diet solutions to lose weight. Why aren't they getting the results they desire? What about business and self improvement seminars? Most of the information people learn at those seminars and in those CD's and books is never applied.

The knowledge is there; make no mistake about that. The question is, does it really give us power if we don't use it?

Many years ago I listened to an interview with Vince Lombardi, who is to this day considered one of the greatest football coaches of all time. Coach Lombardi said something so profound that it still resonates with me today. He said, *"If we are brilliant on the basics, and execute them every time; it will not matter if the opposing team knows what play we are going to run. They will not be able to stop us."*

This is true for any business. When your team knows the basics, and executes them consistently; you will be successful.

I am going to share many different strategies and ideas throughout this book. Most of the information you may already know. If not, you have probably heard it before. What you gain from reading this book will be directly proportionate to how much you apply what you've read, and to how much of that you *take* continuous action on. Remember, knowledge is power ... but only when you apply it consistently.

Barry Gottlieb / Author – Speaker – Trusted Advisor

BUSINESS LANDSCAPE

"Success is neither magical nor mysterious. Success is the natural consequence of consistently applying the basic fundamentals."

Jim Rohn

CHAPTER 1
BUSINESS LANDSCAPE

The former CEO of General Electric, Jack Welch, said the following, "If the rate of change outside your organization is greater than the rate of change inside your organization, the end is near."

The business landscape that we once knew has changed dramatically over the past few decades, and it will continue to change at warp speed. If you are not an agent of change, the future will be very challenging for you and your business.

For example, one of the first things I do when I walk in the door of a company I've been hired to coach is ask about their presence on Facebook, Twitter, or other social media platforms. Most have nothing to show. Others have only just begun to realize the power of social media.

Note that Facebook alone has more than 800 million users. The average user spends between 20 to 30 minutes online every day. What is your company doing to increase its presence on social media? Please keep in mind, the cost to you as a business owner for that presence is zero dollars.

This is just one of the multitude of changes that are shaping the way business is being conducted in today's global economy.

Consider the following statistics:

- A corporation fails every three minutes in America
- 40% of businesses fail within the first year
- 80% of them will be out of business within five years
- 90% will close their doors before their tenth year

These numbers are alarming. What are the main reasons for these failures?

Here are the top five:

- Bad customer relations
- Bad budgeting
- Lack of continuous training
- Failure to anticipate market trends
- Poor and/or inconsistent marketing

In the next several chapters, we will take a close look at each of these top five reasons, and some solutions to prevent them from happening in your company.

WHY BUSINESSES FAIL - REASON #1:

BAD CUSTOMER RELATIONS

*"Do what you do so well that
they will want to
see it again and bring their
friends."*

Walt Disney

CHAPTER 2

WHY BUSINESSES FAIL - REASON #1:
BAD CUSTOMER RELATIONS

The Number One reason you lose a customer is because the customer perceives that you don't care. Be careful, I didn't *say* you don't care. I said the customer *perceives* that you don't care. There is nothing specific that causes a customer to feel this way. It can be anything, and sometimes everything that you do or don't do. This is why it is critical to your business that you recognize how important relationships are in the business process.

You have probably heard this before: People do business with people that they *know*, they *like*, and they *trust*. The question you need to ask yourself is, what are you doing in your organization to make sure that everyone on your team understands the importance of this concept? I believe there is one, most important ingredient in building a successful business. That ingredient is to create a culture within your company that focuses on making the *experience* a customer has a positive, memorable one; every time they deal with your company.

Some experts would disagree. They might say that quality, price, or speed of execution are more important. Each of these are important ingredients in building a successful business. I consider these the entry fee for staying in business. However, keep in mind that each of these ingredients can and will be copied.

On the other hand, creating a culture that in turn creates positive and memorable experiences for your customers, *every* time, will be difficult if not impossible to replicate.

Remember: It is all about the experience! Here are some key points to help you in this area:

- The top 20% of your customers are responsible for approximately 80% of your business.
- Do you know who they are? Do your managers? Do your sales people?

- When was the last time someone from your company visited them?
- When was the last time someone in your company did something to delight or astonish them? (Read the chapter on Customer Service/ Satisfaction)
- Do you know if they are doing more or less business with you than they did last year?
- Do you know the reasons why?
- Have you created an action plan to win that business back?
- Do you have a process to measure the execution of that plan?
- Remember, it is approximately seven times harder to get a customer back than it is to get them to buy initially.
- Does everyone on your team (salespeople, receptionists, management, drivers, clerks, etc.) know how important their role is in delivering a positive experience, *every* time?

WHY BUSINESSES FAIL - REASON #2:

BAD BUDGETING

"You'll fail at 100% of the goals you don't set."

Mark Victor Hansen

CHAPTER 3

WHY BUSINESSES FAIL - REASON #2:

BAD BUDGETING

Most companies don't like to discuss the budget with their employees. They keep it tightly guarded in the inner circle of upper management, then leave it to the managers to make sure their departments meet that budget.

In order for people to hit their targets, they must know what they are aiming for and how to achieve that goal. They should know and understand their role in helping the company achieve its budget.

The number one motivator of peak performance in any individual is knowing what their specific purpose is. When we know what is expected of us, we perform at a much higher level.

There is more to a budget then simply identifying a dollar goal. For example, a sales team should have a budget (goals) identified for each of the following areas:

- Dollars
- Gross Margin %
- New Accounts (to open and sell)
- Contacts ... on a daily and/or weekly basis
- Customer Visits
- Collection Time (number of days)
- Level of Customer Satisfaction

Look at your department and determine those things that will have a direct and indirect impact on achieving your budget (goals).

The key to achieving your budget is to ensure that everyone knows their purpose and how to achieve their individual goals and objectives. Then creating a process to measure the execution of that plan.

WHY BUSINESSES FAIL - REASON #3:

LACK OF STAFF TRAINING

*"Train everyone lavishly; you can't
overspend on training."*

Thomas Peters

CHAPTER 4

WHY BUSINESSES FAIL - REASON #3:
LACK OF STAFF TRAINING

Over 80% of companies do no training after the initial on-boarding when an employee joins the organization.

This is the opposite of what the best teams and individual peak performers do.

Whenever I give a live presentation or seminar, I ask the audience to yell out the name of a winning team. The answers I usually receive are "The Yankees!", "The Lakers!", or the local city's team. Then I ask them to think outside the box of sports. I ask them to yell out names of other peak performing teams. Some of the common answers I hear include astronauts, a symphony orchestra, the Navy Seals, etc.

I am still waiting for the day when someone yells out the name of their company! Did *you* think of your company when I asked that question?

What makes a winning team? What are the qualities, attributes, and characteristics of a winning team or individual? I believe that if you list them all, you will come to the conclusion that I have. These peak performers are absolutely *brilliant on the basics*. How did they get that way? I can assure that the one thing all of these teams do, on a regular, ongoing basis, is train.

They *train*! Not just when they start on the team, the orchestra, the Special Operation's Team; they train on a *consistent* basis.

Sure, the other qualities, attributes, and characteristics matter. But they must be learned, and then they must be practiced over and over again. First, winners memorize the things in which they must excel. Then, over time and with countless hours of practice, they synthesize what they have memorized. This is when it becomes autonomic; when it happens without thinking.

In business, great teams make training part of their standard operating procedures. They train:

- On product knowledge
- On customer knowledge
- On market knowledge
- On the core values of the company
- On the vision and mission of the company

WHY BUSINESSES FAIL - REASON #4:

FAILURE TO ANTICIPATE MARKET TRENDS

"Wisdom consists of the anticipation of consequences."

Norman Cousins

CHAPTER 5

WHY BUSINESSES FAIL - REASON #4:

FAILURE TO ANTICIPATE MARKET TRENDS

Most companies neglect this very important process. They get so caught up in the day to day whirlwind of doing what they have always done. Then before you know it, they have become obsolete.

A shocking example of this is Kodak. We all remember those "Kodak Moments". Kodak has been one of the most recognized brand names in the world. So how is it that they are now in bankruptcy? The simple answer is "digital cameras".

Do you know which company first created digital cameras? The answer may surprise you ... it was Kodak! Instead of recognizing the market trend, unfortunately for them, they decided it would hurt their film business and did not take the idea to market.

The rest is history.

- What do you do in your company to anticipate market trends?
- Are you proactive ... or reactive?
- Do you make decisions based upon emotion, or do you use analytical data and business intelligence?
- Do you survey your customers, or do you assume you know what they want and need to be successful?
- Have you and your team mastered the "art of asking questions"?

WHY BUSINESSES FAIL - REASON #5:

POOR &/OR INCONSISTENT MARKETING

"Make it simple. Make it memorable. Make it inviting to look at. Make it fun to read."

Leo Burnett

CHAPTER 6

WHY BUSINESSES FAIL - REASON #5:

POOR AND/OR INCONSISTENT MARKETING

Marketing is one of the key components of a successful business. Here are the 7 P's of Marketing:

People

- Who is your customer?
- Are they male, female, young, old, etc.?

- Is your sales representative / account executive / consultant a good match?
- Do you have a detailed Customer Profile for every one of your customers or clients?

Product

- What are you selling?
- Most customers or clients want to know what you and your product or service will do for them, rather than what you are selling.

Price

- Remember, selling based on price alone is a downward spiral and it drives most companies out of business.
- There will always be someone that can cut your price.
- When was the last time you visited an Apple retail store? They are not only financially successful, they are ranked as one of the best places to shop and to work; and their products are anything but cheap.

Packaging

- Perceived value plays a major role in the success of your product or business.
- This is relevant throughout every phase of your business, not just in how you package your product.

- How do your employees look when they are face to face, dealing with a customer?
- How about your delivery people?
- What does your facility look like to your customers?
- How about your website, brochures, and flyers?
- What is your IMAGE?

Promotion

- How do you promote your company and your product?
- Which of the following media do you use?
- Radio
- Television
- Magazines / Newspaper
- Word of Mouth
- Social Media

Positioning

- Identify your customer's hot buttons, then push them.
- To do this, you must first fully understand your customer.
- What are their needs?
- Why is your product the best solution to satisfy their needs?
- What are they looking for?
- Speed of delivery

- Unique products
- Quality
- Legendary Service
- Price

Placement

- Where will you place your product?
- Storefronts
- Trucks
- Billboards
- Banner ads on the Internet
- Where else?

CLARITY IS THE KEY

*"If we could see the miracle of a single flower
clearly, our whole life would change."*

Buddha

CHAPTER 7
CLARITY IS THE KEY

Jack Welch once said, "*An 'A' leader is a man or a woman with a vision, and the ability to articulate that vision so powerfully and vividly that it becomes the vision of the team.*"

As a leader in a company, you must understand the vital importance of "clarity".

The Number One motivator of peak performance in any individual is their understanding of precisely, specifically, their purpose. They clearly know what they are expected to do, what their goals are, and what their results should be.

They also know how to achieve those goals and objectives, and how to measure them.

I am constantly surprised and disappointed by how many companies have mission statements that look great on the wall or the desk in the reception area. Yet the vast majority of the employees cannot recite it. In most cases, neither can the CEO or company President!

Your company's mission and vision statement should be concise and memorable. It should resonate with both your employees and your customers.

One of the key elements to executing the plans and strategies that you have defined with clarity, is to create a method to systematically measure the execution of the plan.

Without this key element, roughly 80% of even the best plans will fail.

TWO WAYS TO INCREASE PROFITS

"In the end, all business operations can be reduced to three words: people, product, and profits. Unless you've got a good team, you can't do much with the other two."

Lee Iacocca

CHAPTER 8

TWO WAYS TO INCREASE PROFITS

Quite simply, there are only two ways that I know of for a company to increase their profits.

- Increase revenues!
- Cut costs!

Yes, there are many different ways under these two categories to achieve profit in a company. The truth though, is that everything falls under one of these two umbrellas.

As a leader in your company, you must always be laser focused on these two areas. Everyone that works with you should be as well. Here is a simple method to help you and your management team stay laser focused. It is called, "Would You...?"

If you were starting a brand new company, "Would you...?"

(Note: Answers must be a simple "yes" or "no". There is no discussion as to why, and "maybe" is unacceptable.)
"Would you...?"

- Hire the people who are currently working with you? (Have the manager of each department go through their list of staff.)
- Buy from your current suppliers and vendors?
- Offer the same payment plan?
- Use the same insurance company?
- Sell to all of your current customers or markets?
- Etc., etc.

When it comes to the members of your team, if the answer is "no", then the immediate follow up question should be, "Is this something that can be fixed through training and education?" If the answer to this question is "yes", then take immediate action to make that happen.

If the answer to any of the "Would you...?" questions is still a no, then take immediate action to make the changes that are obvious.

How can you expect your company to grow and prosper if you have managers, staff, vendors, suppliers, or policies that you would not choose if you were starting a new company tomorrow?

These decisions are difficult, but you owe it to yourself and to the employees who are adding value, to make these changes immediately. For best results, this exercise should take place quarterly.

DIFFERENT FROM
AND
BETTER THAN

*"You have to learn the rules of
the game, and then
you have to play better than
anyone else."*

Albert Einstein

CHAPTER 9

DIFFERENT FROM AND BETTER THAN

What makes you different from, or better than, your competition? What makes your company different from, or better than, your competitors?

If you don't know the answers to these questions, and if your customers or clients don't know the answers to these questions, then you only have one thing to compete with; and that is price. As you already know, price is usually a downward spiral.

If you have to think about the answers to these questions, then you are not properly prepared or properly trained. Start by taking a personal inventory of why someone should want to do business with you. How do they benefit by dealing with you, or your company?

Start by looking at the features and benefits of your product or your service, and your company. Make sure you and your team know what they are. Make sure that these features and benefits are written and regularly discussed internally. Have your management team practice sharing your product's or service's features and benefits with one another, so they can smoothly "sell" them to your customers or clients. They do not have to be things that are exclusive to you or your company. What is important is that you know them, and that you are sharing them with your customers or clients.

Customers and clients don't necessarily want to know what your product or service is. What they really want to know is what it will do for them.

Here is an example of a company selling their features and benefits, rather than selling their product. Many years ago, American Express ran a full page ad in several national news publications. The ad was very simple and to the point. It stated:

"If you are an American Express card member and your card is lost or stolen, and there are unauthorized charges applied to your card; you don't have to worry, you won't be billed for those charges."

Now, Visa and MasterCard have always provided the same benefit, but there was a difference. They were selling their cards to the consumer, while American Express was selling the features and benefits of being a card member.

There are many companies that share similar products. What the winning companies do is focus on the features and benefits of their product, rather than on the product itself.

This is one of the key strategies for making your company different from, and better than your competition.

THE FOUR GUIDING PRINCIPLES

"If you want to achieve excellence, you can get there today. As of this second, quit doing less-than-excellent work."

Thomas J. Watson, Sr.

CHAPTER 10
THE FOUR GUIDING PRINCIPLES

When I left teaching at the University of Florida to enter the world of business, I quickly realized that I needed to become a student all over again. I knew absolutely nothing about creating a successful, profitable business. So I set out to learn the best practices and the best principles of the best run companies in the world.

Through countless hours of seminars, audio programs, and video programs I was able to learn what the best companies in the world were doing to become the leaders in their respective fields.

I then took the information I learned and applied it in our new company. The most important lesson I learned is that you don't have to reinvent the wheel; you just have to benchmark what the best are doing, and then make it your own.

The true benefits:

- My learning curve was dramatically reduced.
- I implemented strategies I may never have thought of before.
- I found out how important it is to have mentors and coaches. All the peak performers and the best teams in the world have them.
- Now... So did I.
- The lessons are invaluable.

One of the key lessons I learned and applied came from Francis "Buck" Rogers. Buck was the VP at one of the best companies in the world at that time, IBM. In his book, he wrote about three core areas on which everyone at IBM was focused. These three areas became part of the Four Guiding Principals of my new business.

Guiding Principle #1: Commitment to Excellence

This principle is self-explanatory. It means that everyone in your company must be *completely* committed to excellence. It also means that everything you do in your company, from your product and your service, to your quality and your people; must *always* be: The Best!

The focus of our team was on "excellence". The interesting thing is that when everyone is focused on excellence, on doing things to the best that they can be done, you will hit your budget. When you only focus on a number, you often lose sight of what it takes to hit that number.

Guiding Principle #2: Dedication to Service

Start by understanding that in today's global economy, there is no room for second rate service. Remember, the customer can fire anybody in your organization simply by choosing to buy somewhere else. You can have the best product in the world, but if you don't have the service to enhance that product, your longevity in business will meet an abrupt end.

Guiding Principle #3: Constant Innovation

If you are from my generation, you were raised to believe, "If it ain't broke, don't fix it". This philosophy is a dangerous one to follow in these changing times. I believe you would be better off following a philosophy of, "If it ain't broke, *break* it"!

In today's competitive environment, every company should be challenging its employees to be looking for new ideas, new strategies, new technology, and new ways to reach and take care of their customers. Jack Welch summed it up best, "If the rate of change outside your organization is greater than the rate of change inside your organization, then the end is near."

Constant innovation should a priority for your company, and for you.

Guiding Principle #4: Respect for the Individual

The fourth guiding principle was shared with me by my father. One of the greatest lessons he taught me was the following. He said, *"Son, you don't judge a man by the way he treats the president of a company. You should judge a man by the way he treats the cleaning crew."*

The previous three guiding principles have very little value if they are not combined with respect for the individual. People are the greatest asset of any business. How we treat the people that we do business with, and the people that work with us, is one of the KEY elements for success.

SUCCESS VERSUS SURVIVAL

*"Success is doing ordinary things
extraordinarily well."*

Jim Rohn

CHAPTER 11

SUCCESS VERSUS SURVIVAL

If you are a winner, and you are really good at what you do; what would you do if your employer told you that the company was in survival mode?

If it were me, I would get my resume together and start my search for a company that is in success mode. How about you? What would *you* do?

Why would a leader or manager ever plant that awful seed in the minds of their employees? I know some of you might believe that by saying these words, you would be inspiring your team to work harder and produce better results. But isn't there an implied "or else" to the statement of being in survival mode?

Winning companies and winning individuals are focused on success. Period. Even in challenging economic times.

I will give you an example. Let's say that ten years ago, the universe of your business could be represented by a pie. This pie represented the entire potential for sales between your company and your competitors. We'll say that your company's slice of that business represented 10% of the entire pie.

Now fast forward to today. Imagine that the overall size of the pie has diminished by 15%. You have felt it in your business, and so have many of your competitors. Most companies fall into the trap of focusing on how much the pie has shrunk. Most of them have gone into survival mode.

You, however, are better than that. You fully recognize that even though the overall size of the pie has gotten smaller, there is still plenty of pie out there that you never had before. Your company goes into success mode. You start an aggressive plan to take market share (more pie) from your competitors. They are so busy preaching survival while you are focused on success, that your company grows while theirs shrink.

This is what winners do consistently. They *always* focus on success.

• Avoid trying to buy the pie by lowering prices; this is a downward spiral.

- Focus on helping your customers grow their business.
- Find out what their top challenges are, and help your customers solve them.
- Focus on your features and your benefits, rather than on price.
- Provide world class, legendary customer service.
- Delight and astonish the top 20% of your customer base; they are your lifeline.
- Go after the "A" and "B" customers of your competitors; they like dealing with winners.
- Show them all how much you "care"!

FOCUS ON FOUR FACTORS

*"An ounce of action is worth a ton
of theory."*

Ralph Waldo Emerson

CHAPTER 12
FOCUS ON FOUR FACTORS

Former Member of Congress Ed Foreman is another one of my mentors. I attended a three day workshop years ago presented by Ed called *The Successful Life Course*, which I remember to this day. The course had been featured on 60 Minutes. It was one of those rare times when the story line was positive rather than a negatively skewed piece about a company or a person.

The course was amazing! I learned so many things that helped me both professionally and personally. The most important lesson that I learned was this statement that Ed repeated over and over again throughout the course of the workshop.

"Winners develop the habit of doing the things that losers don't like to do."

To be successful in business, we must recognize that most people and most companies (our competitors) are challenged on a daily basis by the 3 C's (see Chapter 14).

If you want to be different from, and better than, your competition, you must create a culture that is focused on the right things. Develop the habit of focusing on these four areas.

The Four Focus Factors

- **Results**: All leaders must focus on the results they want to achieve. They must also make sure that everyone on the team is aware of them.
- **Solutions**: To achieve these results, you must be focused on solutions rather than challenges. You must create a culture that is always looking at "how" to do it, rather than a culture that only sees the obstacles.
- **Action**: The first two areas of focus will be worthless if all you do is define the desired results and determine how you are going to achieve them. You must take immediate action! This includes determining who is going to be responsible (take ownership), and when it will be successfully completed.
- **Measure**: Approximately 80% of plans fail. They do not fail because the plan was faulty, nor do they fail due to a lack of talent. They usually fail because there is no process and procedure in

place to measure the execution of the plan on a regular, ongoing basis. This is critical to the success of any plan you have. Most companies wait until the end of the quarter, and then look at the results. By then, it is too late to change anything!

Managing with an eye on these Four Factors, and doing them consistently, will drive you toward more profitable results.

FOUR QUESTIONS YOU SHOULD ASK YOURSELF

"It is never crowded on the extra mile."

Wayne Dyer

CHAPTER 13
FOUR QUESTIONS YOU SHOULD ASK YOURSELF

As your relationship with your clients grows, so will your piece of the pie. Remember, it isn't just about selling your product. It's about understanding why people buy. Nobody wants to be sold anything. But, people love to buy. Remember this and it will serve you well.

To help you maintain your competitive edge, here are four questions that you should ask yourself on a regular basis. By regular basis, I suggest doing this at least once a week. Make time to sit down and ask yourself the following questions:

1. What should I do more of?

- What did I do that worked really well?
- What was the most valuable use of my time?
- What gave me a positive return on my investment in time, energy, or money?

Make note of these activities, and plan to do more of them.

2. What should I do less of?

- What did I spend too much time, energy, and money doing that had little value?
- Were there activities that I should have delegated to someone else?

Once you create this awareness, you will find that you and your team spend more time on the things that really matter. Approximately 20% of our time is spent doing the things that add value, and 80% is wasted on trivial matters. If you can change this percentage by just 10%, imagine the difference it would make to your company's bottom line.

3. What should I start?

- What new ideas or strategies have you heard or read about that may be worth trying?
- What new products or services might help your business grow?

- Have you heard or read anything that made you think, "Hmm, that's a pretty good idea"? Well, now you need to make note of those thoughts, and take immediate action to implement them.

Trying ... changing ... trying again ... changing ... That is how great discoveries and successes are made.

4. What should I stop doing?

- What are the things I am doing that are nonproductive, wasting my time, irritating, or add no value?
- Stop doing them, but have an awareness of what they are and if they need to be delegated before you stop doing them all together.
- If they are a waste of everybody's time, then just stop doing them.

BEWARE OF THE 3 C'S

*"Any fool can criticize, condemn and complain;
and most fools do."*

Benjamin Franklin

CHAPTER 14
BEWARE OF THE 3 C'S

The rewards in life and in business are for finding the solutions, not for identifying the problems.

Unfortunately, we live in a society where people thrive on the 3 C's. They love to *condemn, criticize, and complain*. Most research states that approximately 80% of our thoughts are negative in content.

Do you realize how difficult it is to run a profitable, successful business when people focus on what went wrong, who was at fault, why we shouldn't have done what we did, how we should have never tried it in the first place, and who is to blame?

All of this wasted energy complaining and criticizing, and condemning! Does it really make things better? Does it get us moving forward again in a positive direction; or does it just make matters worse?

Let's take an example: A customer receives the wrong product. Does your company immediately look for solutions to make things better? Or do they waste valuable time, energy, and positive morale stuck in the 3 C's mode?

Winners understand the power of not getting lured into the 3 C's. They immediately look for ways to solve the situation or the challenge. They put their energy into focusing on solutions.

Creating a **solution based culture** rather than allowing a 3 C's culture to exist in your company will have a cumulative, positive effect on morale, productivity, and profits!

HOW TO HIRE AND HOW TO FIRE

*"You don't have to be great to start, but you
have to start to be great."*

Zig Ziglar

CHAPTER 15

HOW TO HIRE AND HOW TO FIRE

The Number One reason you lose a customer is that your customer perceives you don't care.

Remember, people like to do business with people that they know, that they like, and that they trust. It is all about relationships, and the more you build positive and strong relationships, the better off your company will be.

Be sure to choose your people with care. Proper selection is vitally important. One of the key attributes of a good leader is selecting the right people.

Only kind, caring, passionate, and overall nice people can deliver astonishing service. There is no other way, because these attributes are almost impossible to teach. When it comes down to who to hire, you should always consider whether the candidate has the characteristics, qualities, and attributes of a winner.

Mac Anderson, author and founder of Simple Truths, says it best in his book, *"You Can't Send a Duck to Eagle School"*. He writes, *"If your company mission is to climb a tree, which would you rather do: Hire a squirrel or train a horse?"*

Here are some very simple rules for hiring:

- Always be interviewing. Even if there are currently no openings in your company, you should always be searching for winners.
- Always interview a candidate you think has potential a minimum of three different times.
- Involve other members of the team in the interview process.
- Have a potential candidate spend a minimum of one hour just wandering around the company; this gives you and your team a chance to see if they fit in (and they get to see if your team is a fit for them).
- Make sure there is clarity regarding the job description; have it written and prepared for them to take with them.

Here are some very simple rules for firing:

- Remember the golden rule: "Hire slowly ... Fire quickly".
- If an employee steals from you, destroys property or hurts others, fire them immediately.
- If an employee simply turns out not to be the right person for a particular job and there is no job available for which they would be a better fit, then "dehire" them. They were hired for a particular job and it did not work out, so let them go compassionately. When letting someone go, do everything possible to preserve their self-esteem.
- Getting into the details of why you are letting them go usually benefits no one. It certainly does not benefit you, even though you feel the need to get it off your chest (that should have happened a long time ago in their quarterly reviews). The best way is to simply state, "I don't feel that you are the right person for this job, and I believe we are not the right company for you." When they ask for details, simply repeat the previous statement.
- The best time to let someone go is usually the first time you think about it.
- Dehire anyone who does not buy into the core values and the mission of the company, *even* if they have the numbers.

THE NUMBER ONE ROLE OF MANAGEMENT

"If you want to gather honey,
don't kick
over the beehive."

Dale Carnegie

CHAPTER 16
THE NUMBER ONE ROLE OF MANAGEMENT

GET RESULTS!

THE NUMBER ONE RULE OF MANAGEMENT

"Effective leadership is putting first things first. Effective management is discipline, carrying it out."

Stephen Covey

CHAPTER 17
THE NUMBER ONE RULE OF MANAGEMENT

Inspect what you expect!

Even the best made plans in business don't always work out. In fact, approximately 80% of plans fail.

Most of those plans did not fail because the plan was flawed. Nor did they fail due to a lack of talented people.

They failed because there was no method or process for measuring the execution of the plan.

Too often, managers wait until the deadline for the completion of a plan to inspect the results. Unfortunately, by this time there isn't anything that can be done to change the outcome. It is imperative that a system be created to measure the ongoing process of any plan or project.

There is an old saying, *"What gets measured, gets done!"*

Here is an example. If your plan is to increase the number of contacts that your sales people have with their customers (something you should all have), you should set a clearly defined, written, and specific goal for each salesperson. If you wait until the end of the month or the end of the quarter to review how they have done, you will be disappointed with the results.

If you **inspect what you expect** on a daily basis, you will ensure the achievement of your goal.

Here is something else to consider.

Too often, managers tell people on their teams what the plan is and they believe their job is done. What they don't realize is that:

- 25% of the people did not understand the plan
- Another 25% don't know how to execute the plan

It is extremely important for managers to make sure that everyone on the team knows the plan, knows how to execute the plan; and understands how important it is for them to measure the execution of the plan on a consistent basis.

THE 6 P'S

"A man who does not think and plan long ahead will find trouble right at his door."

Confucius

CHAPTER 18
THE 6 P'S

How much planning do you do?

Most people spend more time planning a vacation or a party than they do planning their lives or their professional activities.

Most people fail to plan.

They come to work and dive right into doing what they always do. The Franklin Covey Group, one of the top training companies in the world, did extensive research on time management. They found that most people come to work and get sucked into a whirlwind. The whirlwind encompasses all those things they deal with, coming from every direction, all day long. Research shows that up to 80% of those whirlwind activities are trivial in nature.

So as little as 20% of an employee's time is spent on the things that are vital and crucial to the success of the company.

The 6 P's

1.Prior
2.Planning
3.Prevents
4.Piss
5.Poor
6.Performance

Remember: One hour of planning can save up to ten hours of doing what is unnecessary.

Failing to plan ... is planning to fail.

CUSTOMER SERVICE AND CUSTOMER SATISFACTION

"The goal as a company is to have customer service that is not just the best, but legendary."

Sam Walton

CHAPTER 19
CUSTOMER SERVICE AND CUSTOMER SATISFACTION

This is the most important chapter in this book.

Being *Brilliant on the Basics* in all the other core areas of your business won't get you where you want to be if you are not brilliant when it comes to taking care of your customers.

Study these quotes from some of the top business gurus of this century:

* *"There is only one boss: the Customer; and he can fire everybody in the company from the chairman on down, simply by spending his money somewhere else."*
- Sam Walton

* *"America is ripe for a service revolution."* - Harvey Mackay

* *"Quality in service is not what you put into it, it is what the client gets out of it."* - Peter Drucker

* *"Being on par in terms of price and quality only gets you in the game. Service wins the game."* - Tony Alessandra

* *"Customer satisfaction is worthless. Customer loyalty is priceless."* - Jeffrey Gitomer

* *"Customer service is just a day in, day out, ongoing, never ending, unremitting, persevering, compassionate type of activity."* - Leon Gorman

Do these quotes describe your company?

If you answered "Yes", congratulations! You are going to be successful in business for a very long time. You get it, and so do the people that work with you.

If you responded with a no, then it is time to take your company to the next level.

Imagine a ladder of success leaning against the wall in your business...

The bottom rung of that ladder is the step where you **meet your customer's expectations**. At this level, you will struggle to hold onto your customers, let alone take market share away from your competitors. If this is all you strive for, chances are your competitors will steal market share from you.

The second rung of the ladder is a step up. At this level, you are starting to **exceed the expectations of your customers**. This level is still not going to build customer loyalty. If one of your competitors can offer something similar or less expensive, your customers will change direction immediately. They will not feel you are doing anything out of the ordinary, and they will easily be swayed to take their business elsewhere.

The third rung up the ladder is when you really start to separate yourself from your competition. At this level, you are **delighting your customers**. You have connected with them on a personal, emotional level. They look at you as more than a supplier or vendor. They perceive you as a friend; someone that they now know, that they like, and that they can trust. At this level, they know that you truly care about their success, and that you see your relationship as a win-win.

The top rung of the ladder is where you **completely astonish your customer** by displaying both a personal and professional level of commitment that is truly rare and unique. At this level, you are not only making your customer feel like a valued friend, you are proving that you are a valued and trusted advisor. You not only show that you care, but your execution on everything you have promised the customer is flawless. At this level, you will never have to worry about someone stealing your market share from you.

CUSTOMER OR CLIENT PROFILES

"There is a place in the world for any business that takes care of its customers... After the sale."

Harvey Mackay

CHAPTER 20

CUSTOMER OR CLIENT PROFILES

Most of the companies I have coached over the past decade did not have formal profiles on their customers or clients. Some didn't have them because they never even thought about the benefit. Others heard there were benefits, but never made it a priority. How about your company?

What if I told you that having detailed customer or client profiles would have a positive impact on your bottom line? Would you be interested in creating them for your company? Do you remember the Number One reason that we lose a customer? I shared it with you back in Chapter 2; that the customer perceives that you don't care. Customer or client profiles force you and your team to learn and remember more about them.

Many companies have information about their customer's or client's buying habits. This information is important to have and to know, but it is not what makes that customer or client loyal or faithful. Remember, people do business with people that they know, like and trust. The more you know about your customer, the closer they perceive you to be not just a vendor, but a friend.

I'll share a brief story about one of our customers at our import company. We made it mandatory that customer profiles be filled out and updated on a regular basis. If you were to bring a customer up on the computer, the system would automatically take you to their customer profile.

One of the categories that was required (if at all possible) was to obtain the birth date of the customer (just date, not year). We had a rule that all customers were to be sent a birthday card from their account representative. Often times, managers would also sign the cards.

One day I received a phone call from one of our top 20 customers. He called to say how grateful he was that our account representative had sent him a birthday card. He went on to tell me that when he was leaving for work and said goodbye to his wife, she neglected to mention his birthday. He then went on to tell me that when he got to his store, his two sons who worked with him had *also* made no mention of his birthday. But there, sitting on his desk was the card from our company; signed by most of the sales team and managers, wishing him a happy birthday. Needless to say, he was very grateful and viewed us as more than just a supplier. To this customer, we were friends. When you build this kind of relationship it is very difficult for one of your competitors to take market share away from you.

If you would like to see an example of a world class customer profile, simply Google "Mackay 66".

Make the use of Customer or Client Profiles a winning habit in your company. You will be glad you did, and so will your customers.

THE FIVE RULES OF SELLING

"For every sale you miss because you're too enthusiastic, you will miss a hundred because you're not enthusiastic enough."

Zig Ziglar

CHAPTER 21
THE FIVE RULES OF SELLING

Every sales team I have managed or coached over the years has been required to learn these Five Rules of Selling. These rules are the basics. If your team is brilliant on these basics, they will, *absolutely,* blow away the competition.

The first step is to make sure that every member of the team memorizes The Five Rules. Once this is complete, you can work on the training that will help them incorporate The Five Rules into their daily work routines. In other words, they will do The Five Rules without thinking about them. It will become an autonomic response.

Here are **The Five Rules**:

Rule #1: Persistence Breaks Resistance

Most sales people give up after their first attempt. In most cases, it requires a minimum of nine attempts to even have a fighting chance to break through to a new prospect. Sometimes it will take twenty to thirty attempts! The point is, if you have qualified this prospect and you know they are worth your time, don't give up. No matter how many times you have to try.

Rule #2: The Sale Begins When the Customer Says "No"

If a customer or client calls and asks you for your product or service, this is not selling. This is taking an order. A sale truly begins when you ask the customer or client to buy something, and they say, "No". What you do after that to get them to buy, is selling.

Rule #3: Ask For the Sale

As you read that statement, you probably thought, "Well, everyone does that all the time!" Unfortunately, you are wrong. I have studied thousands of sales people in numerous industries, and I have learned that most people neglect this vital step. Yes, they have wonderful conversations with their prospects, and they certainly build rapport. They often fill the requests or orders given by their customers. But in most situations, they miss the opportunity to "close" a true sale simply because they do not ask for it!

Rule #4: Ask For More

One of the easiest ways to increase your sales and your profits is to create the habit of always asking for more. One out of every three times that you ask for more; you will get an additional sale. This rule alone will increase your revenues dramatically.

I will give you a brief example. Have you ever gone through the drive-through at Wendy's? When you reach that little speaker box, the first thing you hear is, "Would you like to try our new fish sandwich combo today?" (or whatever they are pushing on that particular day). When you respond with, "No thank you, I would like a #1 Combo with a Coke.", they immediately ask if you would like a large or a medium. You may not even realize that you have just been "asked for more"! You respond with either "large" or "medium". The fact is, the #1 Combo comes with a small drink and a small fry! Can you imagine how much extra revenue Wendy's has generated by using this single, simple technique?

This doesn't happen every once in a while at Wendy's or McDonald's. This is part of their culture, their training. These corporations have hired experts to help them understand how to influence how people buy. You will never hear that employee at Wendy's ask if you would like to leave it as an order of a small coke and fries. They know that people always move toward their current, dominant thought. They make additional revenue every day just by training their employees to ask that simple question.

How can you make this happen in your company?

Rule #5: Selling Is Not Telling, Selling Is Asking Questions

If you have a meeting with a prospective customer and you spend forty-five minutes talking, and they only speak for fifteen minutes; when you leave they are going to think, *"Well, that guy was okay, but I couldn't wait for that to end"*. On the other hand, if you get the prospect to talk for forty-five minutes and you only speak for fifteen; the customer is going to think, *"Wow, that guy was great! He really cared about me and my business".*

The last thing you want to do is *"tell sell"* your customer on your product or your company. Instead, you should want to ask questions to understand who they are, what their greatest challenges are, how their business is doing, what they like about their current vendors, what don't they like, whether they like their job, if they are the decision maker, if they are not, then who is ... the list goes on and on.

Once you have gathered enough information, also known as *profiling* your prospect or customer; you will be in a much better place to offer solutions that will help them to overcome their challenges.

Two of my favorite questions to ask new prospects as well as existing customers are, *"What are the two* greatest challenges you face in your job today?", and "What is the greatest challenge your company faces right now?".

Please note that when you ask these questions, you are not expected to provide a solution; your job is to be a great listener.

After your conversation, write notes about what was said and what you learned. Later, if you gain some information or identify a solution to those challenges you can contact the individual and share what you have learned.

For example, you might read an article that pertains to a challenge that was shared. Then simply copy and forward the article with a note saying how it reminded you of your conversation and thought it would be helpful to share.

It is *all* about building relationships. Remember the Number One reason you lose a customer is because they perceive that you don't care. The best way to build a long lasting relationship is for them to know that you *do* care.

Become a master of the art of asking questions!

THE SIXTH RULE OF SELLING

"Sales are contingent upon the attitude of the salesman; not the attitude of the prospect."

W. Clement Stone

CHAPTER 22
THE SIXTH RULE OF SELLING

"WOOBAH DAHBAH"...

HAVE FUN!!!

HOW TO HANDLE OBJECTIONS

"One who gains strength by overcoming obstacles possesses the only strength which can overcome adversity."

Albert Schweitzer

CHAPTER 23
HOW TO HANDLE OBJECTIONS

We all face objections and challenges on a regular basis. Objections come in all shapes and sizes. They can be about a product, price, service, the company, or many other areas.

There are four basic steps that you should apply when faced with an objection. Once you've mastered these steps you will be able to take almost any objection and turn it into a positive experience; both for the customer and for your company.

Step One: Request further information
This could be as simple as saying, *"Please tell me more"*, or *"Can you share a few more details with me?"*,

or *"Is there anything else?"*. In other words, when some-one has an objection, your first step is to get them to tell you everything. Your goal is to allow them to let it all out.

Step Two: Hear Them Out / Listen Respectfully

Once you have requested additional information, you must become an expert listener. Most of us have the tendency to believe we have "the" answer, and interrupt when somebody has an objection (i.e., a complaint or a challenge) and we've asked them to tell us more about it. We might say something like, *"No, no, no, we don't have to do it that way; we can do it this way..."*. We don't let them get it all out. One of the most important things we can do when dealing with an objection is to allow the other person to finish what they have to say. We must learn to hear them out, and wait for them to finish speaking.

Step Three: Play Back What You Believe You Heard Them Say

This shows the other person that you were listen-ing, and that you *do* care. You might say, *"If I heard you correctly, you are upset because..."* This gives them the opportunity to let you know that you fully understand what they perceive the problem to be. If you didn't get it right, they will explain the piece you are miss-ing (again, listen respectfully). This builds respect and trust.

Step Four: Offer Solutions

Now that you fully understand the challenge, you have the opportunity to present solutions and offer points that will support your position. If you don't have a clear, exact solution, you might say, *"I regret that you had this problem. What can I do to make this right?"*. Remember: The customer may not always be right, but they always want to feel like they won.

GOALS

"The reason most people never reach their goals is that they don't define them, learn about them, or even seriously consider them as believable or achievable. Winners can tell you where they are going, what they plan to do along the way, and who will 'take ownership'."

Denis Waitley

CHAPTER 24
GOALS

The Number One motivator of peak performance is when people know clearly and specifically what their purpose is; their goals. Conversely, the Number One de-motivator is when people do not have a very clear expectation of what they are responsible for, their purpose, or their goals.

Did you know that only about 5% of people have *clearly defined, written, specific goals*?

Here are the basic rules for setting and achieving your goals. Remember, a dream or a wish is the way you would like your world to be. A goal is what you intend to make happen.

Step One: Goals Must be in Writing

They should be written in the *first person, in present tense, and they must be positive.* Here are a few examples:

- Instead of saying, *"I need to lose 20 pounds", you should say, "I am a lean, fit, healthy __ pounds".* (Insert your goal.)
- Instead of saying, *"I want to make $50,000 this year", you should say, "I earn $50,000 a year."*

Step Two: Identify the Obstacles

Obstacles are what you are going to have to overcome, to achieve your goals. This should also be done in writing.

Step Three: List Your Resources

Make a list of the resources that you may need to help you overcome your obstacles. This may include people, equipment, data, etc.

Step Four: Set a Time Frame

Establish when you will accomplish your goal. This may be short term, intermediate, or long term. This is a critical step. Without a time frame, you will most likely not accomplish your goals.

Step Five: First Action Step

List what your first action step is going to be, and when you are going to take it.

Step Six: Measuring the Execution of Your Plan

Create a **process and procedure to measure** the execution of the plan.

TIME MANAGEMENT

"Until you value yourself, you will not value your time. Until you value your time, you will not do anything with it."

M. Scott Peck

CHAPTER 25
TIME MANAGEMENT

You can always earn more money, but you cannot earn more time! One of the most important skill sets you need to master to achieve the level of success you desire, is time management. Yet 80% of the people in our country have very poor time management skills, if any. We hear people say all the time, *"There is simply not enough time in the day".*

The truth is, time is the one factor that we all share in common. Each day has 24 hours, no matter where you work or who you are. In this area, the playing field is always level. How you use your time is an altogether different story. People with good time management skills accomplish more, and stand out in any company.

Here is a simple formula for creating great time management skills:

- Before you leave work at the end of the day, set aside ten minutes to create your **"To Do"** list for tomorrow (your goals) on a small Post-It Note or in a notepad.
- Your To Do list should have on it the one to three tasks that you are going to accomplish the next day.
- The maximum number of items on your list should never exceed three. Studies have proven that if you have up to three things on your list, you will most likely accomplish all of them. If you have four to ten things on your To Do list, you will probably only accomplish two of them. If you have ten to twenty things on your list, you will probably not accomplish any of them (So follow the guideline, only list up to three).
- You may keep a Master List (this "Wish List" is not your To Do list) of *all the* things you hope to get done or wish you could accomplish in the short term. This list can include as many items as you want. The difference is, a wish is what you hope you will get done. A goal is what you intend to make happen.
- Choose one to three items that will have the greatest value for you and your company.

- Be sure to choose the items that are the most important, rather than the most urgent.
- Ask yourself this question, *"If I could pick one thing that would be the best use of my time and have the greatest, positive return on my investment of time and energy; what would that one item be?"* Write it down.
- Then repeat this step two more times until you have identified your list of three tasks.
- When you come in the next day, review your list.
- Start with the most important task and stay laser focused on it until you complete it.
- Check it off your list and move on to number 2, and then number 3.

Here is some additional advice. The average worker gets interrupted approximately seven times an hour (by other people, emails, text messages, and the phone). Along with the formula above, you must learn to say "No" (Be responsible for you ... Stay in control).

Master this ... and you will achieve things beyond your wildest dreams!

ATTITUDE

"Attitude is a little thing that makes a big difference."

Winston Churchill

CHAPTER 26
ATTITUDE

Everyone has an attitude. Obviously, some are better than others. There are those people who always beam with positive energy, and consequently have a positive effect on those around them.

Then there are those people with negative attitudes. They are the ones that somehow take even the best of circumstances and find some way to put a dark cloud over it.

Even the people that tend to do nothing or have no opinion about things have an attitude... *The attitude to do nothing or be apathetic.*

Research over the past fifty years indicates that your attitude is a key factor in determining your level of happiness and success. These studies also point out the impact of your attitude on your health. When it comes to your success in your career, the research indicates that 85% of the reason a person gets a job, keeps a job, and gets ahead in their job is directly related to their attitude.

To quote Zig Ziglar: *"It is your attitude, not your aptitude, that determines your altitude."*

Think about your own personal experiences in restaurants and retail stores. If you are like me, the attitude of an employee can either make or break the deal. I will not go back to a restaurant where the food was good, but the attitude of the employees was negative. It reflects on the entire experience. Conversely, great service and positive attitudes can make an average place into a memorable experience.

Attitude *does* make a difference.

Consider this: Who would you choose, the doctor that says, "You are the one in a hundred that will survive", or the equally skilled doctor that says, *"Ninety-nine out of a hundred people die from this; your chances aren't very good"?*

The choice is obvious.

What is the attitude culture in your company?

Here are some action steps for you to work on with your team:

- Have the team talk about and agree on someone they consider to be a great role model (past or present).

- Have the team list at least twenty to thirty qualities and characteristics that make that person such a positive role model. (Example: they are honest, trustworthy, caring, have integrity, are kind, consistent, have a strong work ethic, are talented, etc.).
- Now, list next to each one of these characteristics whether it is a skill "S", or an attitude "A" (Example: We are taught to be honest, but honesty is not a skill, it is an attitude … so place an "A" next to it).
- Have the team go through the entire list, with you marking each characteristic as a skill or an attitude.
- When you are done I believe you will find, just like I have in doing this exercise with thousands of people, that approximately 90% of the characteristics get labeled with an "A", for attitude.
- Now, on a scale of 1 to 5, with 5 being excellent; how would you rate *your* attitude?
- How would your friends, coworkers, or employees rate your attitude?
- Ask yourself these questions, and answer them honestly…

  o *Would you want to work with you / for you?*
  o *Would you want to work for a boss like you?*

Remember… Attitudes are contagious! Is yours worth catching?

HOW MUCH ARE YOU WORTH?

"When people believe in them-selves, they have the first secret of success."

Norman Vincent Peale

CHAPTER 27:
HOW MUCH ARE YOU WORTH?

A large percentage of the people I have managed or coached over the years have shared with me their desire (most say their "need") to make more money.

Are you feeling this way as well?

I can honestly tell you that the vast majority of good business owners would be thrilled to pay you more money. All they want in return, is for you to earn it.

So, let me ask you a very simple question, "What are you doing today that you weren't doing last week, last month or last year, to earn more money?"

The fact is, we live in a very competitive global economy. Business today is significantly different than it was five or ten years ago. Remember that nine out of ten companies will fail before their tenth year.

What have you learned and applied in your job that has made a noticeable difference to the bottom line of your company?

Most of the people who have shared their dissatisfaction with their current compensation package have a difficult time telling me (or their boss) what additional value they have added to the company's bottom line.

Here are some **Action Steps** to help you earn more money:

- Start by **working on YOU**! Make it your goal to improve and secure your future, to improve your value.
- **Stop blaming** your boss, the company, your fellow employees, the economy, your dog for eating your homework.
- **Take ownership** of YOU! Be responsible! Be accountable!
- **Improve your level of education** (see if your company offers any assistance).
- **Read more books**. The average person reads less than one book every year.
- **Wake up 15 minutes earlier**. Read something inspirational, educational, motivational, or spiritual. Did you ever stop to think that if you did this five days a week, at the end of the year you would have read perhaps as many as a dozen books?!

- **Listen to audio programs**. You can buy them online or at any bookstore.
- Make your drive to work a **classroom on wheels**. Listen to something that adds value to your life while you drive to work.
- **Attend seminars**. Set a goal to attend at least one every year.
- Find a mentor(s).
- Work harder.
- Work smarter.
- Manage your time better.
- **Focus on your top priorities**. Most people spend only 20% of their time on things that add value and 80% on trivial tasks.
- **Avoid the 3 C's** (condemn ... criticize ... complain).
- Be results, solutions, and action oriented.
- **Plan**! One hour of planning saves ten hours of doing.
- Create a process to **measure** the execution of the plan.
- Remember that winners **make it happen.**

Note:

Less than 5% of the people who read this will consistently follow these action steps, and they will reap the benefits. The other 95% will continue to find someone or something to blame for their misfortune.

The choice is yours.

BUILDING A WINNING CHARACTER

"Character is what you know you are, not what others think you have."

Unknown

CHAPTER 28
BUILDING A WINNING CHARACTER

Have you ever been in a situation where you found yourself in a job that you didn't want to be in? Or where you were given a project to do at work that you really weren't all that excited about, let alone wanted to do?

What choice did you make when you were confronted with these situations? Did you decide to give it your very best? Or did you do just enough, but not really enough, because you knew it wasn't something you cared about or wanted to do?

Too often, people sell themselves short without realizing what they are doing when they settle for a lackluster effort. In reality, they are creating a **character of mediocrity** and laziness.

Then one day, the right job or opportunity comes along, and they find themselves lacking in character to give it their very best.

I know some of you will challenge me and say that under these circumstances people will rise to the occasion.

I would ask you to consider that when you are accustomed to only giving 50%-80% all the time, you will find it difficult to give 100% when you need to.

How many times have you said or heard someone else say, *"You can't change a leopard's spots"*?

In all my years in business, I have known so many people with incredible talent that were lacking in character; and they could not understand why they were not getting the promotion or earning more money. They always looked outside of themselves for the reason, or to place the blame.

You have a choice regarding your character. You have what it takes to do your best consistently. You have the ability to change, and to create the life that you desire and deserve.

Make It Happen

- Remember: Winners develop the habit of doing the things that losers don't like to do.
- Be aware of how you talk to yourself and others.

- Remember that your thoughts become your actions, your actions create your habits, and your habits create your character.
- If you want to change something about your character, start by changing the way you think.
- Create the winning habit of always doing more than you are paid to do.
- Look at each challenge as an opportunity.
- Always do your best.
- Accept change.
- Act on reality.

CHANGE

"When we are no longer able to change a situation, we are challenged to change ourselves."

Victor Frankl

CHAPTER 29
CHANGE

"If the rate of change outside your organization is greater than the rate of change inside your organization; then the end is near." Jack Welch

We live in a global economy and the old paradigms of business have shifted, if not disappeared completely. In today's business world, if you are not constantly looking at new and better ways to conduct business, you will probably be left wondering what went wrong.

Recent studies state that nine out of ten companies will fail within ten years. Eight out of those ten will fail within five years. One study estimated that 52% of the companies doing business today in America will not be here one year from now.

Take a good look at your company. Are you aware of the changing dynamics of this global economy? Are you proactive about creating change, or are you reactive and finding yourself trying to figure out what went wrong?

Winning companies are challenging their employees to come up with new and better ways to build their businesses. They are consistently recognizing and rewarding their teams for identifying, and implementing, new and creative ways to achieve their goals.

Winning companies recognize that the days of a five-year plan are long gone. In today's world, a five-year plan is a waste of time and energy. The rapid increases in technology have eliminated the value of a five-year plan. In today's world, a company needs to be consistently examining their immediate goals, and making the proper adjustments to stay ahead of the competition.

Here is an example of how quickly the world is changing. It took just nine months for Facebook to have one hundred million users. Today, they have over eight hundred million users.

If you don't think you need to reevaluate how you are doing business, you may want to think again. I have seen too many individuals and businesses that refused to recognize the inevitability of the new global marketplace, and their companies and their personal lives have paid the price for their denial.

I suggest you start by being aware. Let go of the denial and the deflection. Accept that change is going to take place, and acknowledge that you have a choice whether or not to participate.

In order for you to effect change, you must first be willing to change.

ABOUT THE AUTHOR

Barry is the father of two children, Briana and Luke; and lives with his wife, Cat in South Florida. His personal mission statement is: *To inspire and empower others to reach their full potential.*

His accomplishments include:

FOUNDER: Founder and President of the *Coaching the Winner's Edge* organization and coaching program. http://www.coachingthewinnersedge.com/

SUCCESSFUL BUSINESS BUILDER: Built a $75 Million international company

SALES EXPERT: Former VP of Sales for a Billion dollar company

COACH/TRUSTED ADVISOR: Both a life coach and a business coach, with a successful practice offering counsel and guidance to individuals and corporations

AUTHOR: *"TGIT(Thank GOD It's Today)"* and *"Every Day Is A Gift"*

RADIO HOST: Former Co-Host of *"The Success Show"*, a one hour talk radio program broadcast in South Florida

WEBISODE HOST: Former Co-Host of a weekly, half hour Internet TV program, *"The Insight"*, that focused on transformation and growth

SPEAKER AND TRAINER: Inspires, coaches, and trains business owners, leaders, employees, and individuals with programs targeted for large and small audiences and corporations

NEWSLETTER PUBLISHER: Founder and publisher of the *"TGIT" (tig-it) Weekly Newsletter (To subscribe, send an email to <u>bgott@bellsouth.net</u> and write "Subscribe" in the subject line)*

Made in the USA
Columbia, SC
15 December 2022